EMBR...
IMPERF...

WOMEN'S STORIES OF TRIUMPH

LIAN WAI BEE

INDIA · SINGAPORE · MALAYSIA

CONTENTS

ACKNOWLEDGMENTS

I am deeply grateful to everyone who has been a part of my journey and has contributed to the creation of this book. Your support and encouragement have meant the world to me.

First and foremost, I want to express my heartfelt gratitude to my late parents, who instilled in me values of perseverance and compassion. Their love and wisdom continue to guide me every day. To my siblings, nieces, and nephews, thank you for your unwavering support and for always cheering me on in this journey called "life."

My deepest gratitude to my mentors and teachers—Blair Singer, Mac Attram, Gerry Robert, and Robert Raymond Riopel. Your guidance and teachings have been invaluable in shaping my understanding and approach life with wisdom. You have challenged me to grow and encouraged me to reach beyond my limits.

To my dear friends: Joyce, Suanne, Wai Ling, and Lolitta, thank you for allowing me the privilege to share your stories in this book. Your courage in facing your own challenges and finding your passion is truly inspiring. Your stories will undoubtedly resonate with many readers and offer hope and strength.

Lastly, to all my friends who have been by my side, thank you for your friendship and for lending a helping hand whenever I needed it. Your support has kept me going through the highs and lows of this journey.

To everyone mentioned here and to those who may not be named but have played a part, your contributions have made this book possible. I am deeply grateful for each of you.

With Heartfelt Appreciation,

Lian Wai Bee

CHAPTER 1

UNDERSTANDING THE CONFIDENCE CONUNDRUM

Exploring the roots of self-doubt and the societal pressures that contribute to it

Breaking down what confidence means and how it affects us in everyday life.

Confidence is a powerful force that shapes how we navigate through life. It's the fuel that propels us forward, allowing us to pursue our dreams and overcome challenges with resilience. But for many women, confidence can feel like an elusive concept, slipping through our fingers when we need it most.

In this chapter, we embark on a journey to unravel the intricacies of confidence and uncover the root causes of self-doubt. We'll explore the tangled web of societal pressures and personal experiences that contribute to the confidence conundrum, shedding light on why so many women struggle to embrace their full potential.

1.1 What is Confidence Anyway?

At its core, confidence is the unwavering belief in oneself and one's abilities. It's that inner voice that whispers, "You've got this," even in the face of uncertainty. When we are confident, *we **stand a little taller, speak a little louder, and pursue our dreams with determination.***

But confidence is more than just a state of mind; it's a skill that can be cultivated and honed over time. It's about recognizing our strengths, acknowledging our worth, and learning to trust ourselves in every situation.

1.2 Where Does Self-Doubt Come From?

Despite our best efforts, self-doubt has a sneaky way of creeping into our thoughts and casting shadows on our confidence. It can stem from a variety of sources, including past failures, negative feedback, and comparisons with others.

Our upbringing and personal experiences also play a significant role in shaping our self-perception. Messages we receive from parents, teachers, and peers can influence how we see ourselves and what we believe we're capable of achieving.

Most of the women do not demonstrate confidence; out of 120 women who spoke, more than 70% reported that self-doubt, or not having enough belief in themselves, their capabilities, or their skills, as the driving factor.

https://hbr.org/2022/12/choose-courage-over-confidence

1.3 The Pressure Cooker: Societal Expectations

In addition to our internal struggles, women face external pressures from society that can erode our confidence and self-esteem. From a young age, we're bombarded with messages about how we should look, act, and behave, often conforming to narrow standards of beauty and success. These expectations are deeply rooted in cultural norms and tradition, shaping the way girls perceive themselves and their capabilities.

Family dynamics play a crucial role in shaping a girl's confidence levels and self-perception. In many Asian households, girls are socialized to prioritize the needs and desires of others above their own. They may be taught to be compliant and accommodating, stifling their ability to assert themselves confidently. Additionally, cultural values such as filial piety and respect for authority can reinforce the idea that girls should defer to others, further perpetuating feelings of self-doubt and inadequacy.

These societal expectations create a breeding ground for insecurity, as women constantly measure themselves against unrealistic ideals. Whether it's the pressure to "have it all" or the fear of falling short of perfection, these expectations can take a toll on our mental health and well-being.

1.4 Media Portrayal and Beauty Standards

The media plays a significant role in shaping girls' perceptions of beauty and self-worth, in the world where physical appearance and beauty standards can have a detrimental impact of girl's self-esteem, where they are bombarded with images of unattainable beauty ideas, leading to feelings of inadequacy and dissatisfaction with their own bodies.

The constant comparison and exposure to idealized images can erode girls' confidence and self-esteem, as they strive to conform to societal standards of beauty.

1.5 Cultural Norms and Assertiveness

In certain cultures, especially Asian, the girls are expected to be modest, humble and deferential. We are socialized to prioritize harmony and avoid confrontation, which can hinder our ability to assert ourselves confidently. The concept of "face" is highly valued in many cultures, creating a reluctance to speak up or assert oneself for fear of causing embarrassment or shame.

Furthermore, the stigma surrounding assertiveness and self-promotion can discourage girls from advocating for themselves and pursuing their goals with confidence. Girls may internalize the message that being assertive is synonymous with being aggressive or confrontational, leading them to suppress their own needs and desires to avoid conflict.

An in-depth psychoanalytical study conducted by Harvard Business Review revealed that when women fail to achieve career goals, leaders are prone to attribute it to a lack of self-confidence. When women demonstrate high levels of confidence through behaviors, such as being extroverted or assertive, they risk overdoing it and, ironically, being perceived as lacking confidence. No matter the outcome, women's lack of career progression is blamed on them, an attack they share with other underrepresented groups. This leads women to beat themselves up, which can weaken self-esteem and, in a downward spiral, further erode self-perceptions of confidence.

bit.ly/4fyCIwm

1.6 Navigating the Path Forward

Despite the challenges we face, there is hope on the horizon. By shining a light on the root causes of the confidence conundrum, we can begin to dismantle the barriers that hold us back. Through self-reflection, self-compassion, and support from others, we can cultivate a deeper sense of confidence that empowers us to embrace our true selves.

In the chapters that follow, we will delve deeper into strategies for boosting confidence at any age. From practicing self-care to challenging limiting beliefs, we'll explore practical techniques for building resilience and reclaiming our power. Together, we'll embark on a journey of self-discovery and empowerment, unlocking the limitless potential that lies within each one of us.

CONFIDENCE
is the ability to feel beautiful,
without needing someone to tell you

– Mandy Hale

CHAPTER 2

EMBRACING IMPERFECTION

Learning to Appreciate and Celebrate Flaws as Integral Parts of Our Unique Identity

In this chapter, we embark on a journey of self-discovery and empowerment as we explore the concept of embracing imperfection and celebrating the unique qualities that make each woman special. We delve into the idea that every woman possesses inherent talents and strengths, and by recognizing and embracing these qualities, we can cultivate a sense of self-worth and confidence.

2.1 Embracing Uniqueness

Every woman is inherently unique, with her own set of talents, passions, and quirks that set her apart from others. It is through embracing this uniqueness that women can begin to appreciate and celebrate their individuality. Instead of striving for perfection, women can learn to embrace their imperfections as part of what makes them who they are.

By recognizing and celebrating their unique qualities, women can cultivate a sense of authenticity and confidence in themselves. Whether it's a talent for art, a passion for storytelling, or a knack for problem-solving, every woman has something special to offer the world.

My journey toward embracing imperfection began in my youth, where I grappled with feelings of inadequacy and self-doubt. As an introverted individual, I often felt pressured to conform to societal standards of extroversion and perfectionism. I felt I am ugly, afraid to speak to strangers and always hide myself. I have lost a lot of words on what I should chat about with people around me.

During my university days and freshly started working, the introvert in me, made me struggle to fit in and felt insecure. I always question whether what I said is correct, am I being stupid to raise certain questions. I looked upon those who are so natural when speaking or even doing a flawless presentation that get so much positive feedback. They became my idol and guiding light as I wanted to be like them.

Thankfully, as I embarked on my journey of self-discovery, realizing that every one of us has our own unique beauty and strength, I began to challenge these unrealistic expectations and embrace imperfection as a natural part of me.

2.2 Celebrating Diversity

Diversity is a fundamental aspect of the human experience, and women are no exception. Women come from diverse backgrounds, cultures, and experiences, each contributing to the rich tapestry of humanity. By celebrating this diversity, women can learn to appreciate the beauty of differences and recognize the value that everyone brings to the table.

Instead of viewing differences as shortcomings, women can learn to see them as strengths. Whether it's a different perspective, a unique skill set, or a contrasting personality trait, diversity enriches our lives and enhances our collective experience.

During this period of introspection, I came to realize that imperfection is not something to be ashamed of, but rather something to be celebrated. I learned to appreciate the unique qualities that make me who I am, my flaws and all. Instead of striving for unattainable perfection, I began to focus on self-acceptance and self-love, recognizing that true beauty lies in embracing our imperfections and celebrating our individuality.

I started the practice of journaling, affirming statements like "I am beautiful, I am intelligent, I am capable, I am unique just as I am, and I can accomplish anything with careful planning." This habit has empowered me to cultivate courage, realign with my life goals, and serve as a much-needed morale boost during moments of doubt.

2.3 Discovering Strengths

Each woman possesses a unique set of strengths and talents that make her special. By taking the time to discover and nurture these strengths, women can unlock their full potential and achieve their goals with confidence.

Whether it's a talent for leadership, a gift for communication, or a passion for creativity, women can leverage their strengths to make a positive impact in their lives and the lives of others. By focusing on what they are good at, women can build self-confidence and self-esteem, knowing that they could succeed in whatever they set their minds to.

Embracing imperfection also taught me the power of vulnerability and authenticity. By allowing myself to be seen and heard, flaws and all, I forged deeper connections with others and cultivated a greater sense of empathy and understanding. I realized that it's okay to be imperfect, to make mistakes, and to falter along the way. In fact, it's these imperfections that make us human and enable us to connect with others on a deeper level.

I took proactive steps to learn self-acceptance and self-love, recognizing that negative comments from others are merely their opinions. In response, I graciously acknowledge them with a "Thank You" and continue forward on my path.

2.4 Cultivating Self-Worth

Embracing imperfection is not about settling for mediocrity; rather, it's about recognizing that our flaws and imperfections are what make us human. By learning to accept and love us for who we are, flaws and all, women can cultivate a sense of self-worth and confidence that is not dependent on external validation.

Instead of seeking approval from others, women can learn to validate themselves and find fulfillment from within. By embracing imperfection and celebrating their unique identity, women can unleash their full potential and live authentically, knowing that they are worthy of love and respect just as they are.

Today, I celebrate my imperfections as badges of honor, reminders of the journey I've traveled and the lessons I've learned along the way. I no longer strive for perfection but rather for authenticity and self-compassion. I embrace my flaws as integral parts of my unique identity, knowing that they contribute to my strength and resilience as an individual.

By embracing imperfection, I have found freedom, joy, and a deeper sense of self-acceptance than I ever thought possible.

In essence, embracing imperfection is a journey of self-discovery and self-acceptance. By recognizing and celebrating the unique qualities that make each woman special, we can cultivate a sense of self-worth and confidence that empowers us to live our lives to the fullest.

Do not allow people to dim your shine because they are blinded.

– Lady Gaga

JANET'S JOURNEY THROUGH HER MOTHER'S STORY

A Tale of Love, Resilience, and Artistic Legacy

Late Janet Lee

A Beautiful Beginning and Unexpected Challenges

"What a beautiful, lively baby she was!" Joyce recalls wistfully with a laugh. Janet, the younger of two siblings, seemed perfectly healthy until one night when she was only eight months old. After coming back from dinner, Joyce went to take a shower while her husband was tasked to look after Janet. In the midst of her shower, Joyce's husband noticed Janet's body stiffening with her eyes rolling up. He quickly ran upstairs, alerting Joyce. "I immediately felt something was wrong," Joyce remembers. "My knowledge of baby care and readings from the book told me that Janet's symptoms seem to indicate that she was having a seizure."

Deeply concerned, we rushed to the nearest clinic, where it was confirmed that Janet was indeed having a seizure. At the clinic, the doctor attributed the cause to a viral infection. "I had my doubts because I was absolutely sure that Janet wasn't ill," Joyce adds, shaking her head in disbelief.

After that incident, Janet enjoyed another peaceful eight months before the seizures returned and became distressingly frequent. "This time, they were quite severe, and I was absolutely terrified," Joyce confides. "She would suddenly collapse, followed by jerks all over."

Frequent visits to doctors yielded no results. Janet underwent numerous tests and was put on various medications, but none were successful in treating her condition. "It was devastating," she admits. "We had to be constantly on edge, watching over her and hoping she wouldn't harm herself."

Navigating School and the Pursuit of Acceptance

When Janet started school at age five, her mother soon noticed that she had learning difficulties. "She couldn't retain what she was taught. She couldn't read a word, but my mother-in-law advised me to be patient. Children develop at different paces, she said. Some just need a little more time." While this was true, Joyce and her husband decided to take Janet to an educational psychologist when she started Standard One, as by then, her learning problem was still there. The educational psychologist felt that her learning could have been affected by the epileptic drugs that she took, as some medications do have side effects that could affect learning. "Give her time," was her advice. "Eventually, she'll catch up with the rest."

Prior to visiting the educational psychologist, finding a school that was willing to accept Janet due to her seizures proved difficult. "Not many schools were willing to take on the responsibility of having an epileptic child as a student," Joyce remarks. Even the school where her sister was in, refused to accept her enrollment. We tried convincing the school that, being seven years older and already in Form 1, her sister was capable of knowing what to do if and when Janet had a seizure. Without much hope and after a long and frustrating search, they finally found a private school that was willing to accept her.

"She was such a lovely little girl, and she loved going to school, but she would often doze off in class and could not catch up with what was being taught at school."

When Janet was nine, nothing changed. During a review with the educational psychologist and discussing the issue with her, they were given two options: (1) leave her where she is and let her find her way, or (2) apply for an OKU card (Orang Kurang Upaya/Person With Disabilities which is what is used to reference someone with "Special Needs") and enroll her in a school that catered for Special Needs. Worried about her vulnerability at school, her parents made the hard decision to register her as a "Special Child" and enrolled her in a government/ public school that also had classes to cater for special needs. "It was a difficult decision," Joyce reminisces. "Janet appeared so neurotypical and full of joy. It was painful to see her being placed in a class with children who had more severe disabilities. But we felt that the environment would be safer for her."

When Janet reached her teenage years, she soon realized that she wasn't progressing as much as her sister and cousins. "On some level, she sensed it, and it saddened her," Joyce recalls. Janet also faced challenges at school. When she was ready for secondary school, she had to move to another school, and here, she was frequently assaulted by one of her schoolmates. "She would come home with bruises". When we went to the school to ask what the school was going to do about it, we were told that the schoolmate who assaulted her did the same to others as well, and there was nothing much they could do. The principal's reply was, "This is a class for special needs. If we expel her, where is she going to go?"

Understanding the situation, Janet was eventually removed from the school. In replacement of formal schooling, Joyce arranged for her to attend private classes instead. "It was a tough period for Janet because she was shuttled from one activity to another. It was also challenging for me because I was coordinating all these activities for her, and I soon realized that not everything suited my daughter." Perhaps it was all this shuffling here and there and also her realization that she was not on par with her sister and cousins that made her feel angry and helpless.

Since she couldn't express her feelings verbally, she started becoming aggressive. Initially, it was her expression of anger to her family members and her pet dog. Eventually, it was toward other people who upset her. There was an incident when she even showed that she was about to fight with a lady over a very trivial matter. This became pretty scary. Joyce frantically went around searching for advice from a psychiatrist. After being on medication for two weeks and having her schedule reviewed and steps taken to manage Janet like any other teenager instead of as a child with special needs, Janet's mood stabilized. Time passed without much progress, i.e., Janet was still illiterate, lacked self-confidence, and was very emotional.

A breakthrough came when Janet turned 16. During a family trip to Australia for her sister's graduation, Joyce consulted two specialists. The child psychologist diagnosed Janet with intellectual disabilities, while another one who specialized in working with children who had learning difficulties suspected that Janet's inability to read and write could be due to her vision issue. "I simply followed the specialist's guidance and went to see someone to work on her vision, and in that very year, my daughter learned how to read and write," Joyce shares. "Janet had a passion for learning, and I finally found someone who could tell me what was holding her back!"

Discovering Arts as Therapy and Triumph

Over the years, when Janet struggled to learn and Joyce recognize Janet's interest in coloring, Joyce tried to enroll her in art classes. Unfortunately, after approaching five teachers to give her art lessons, all of them concluded that Janet wasn't a 'gifted artist,' as she had difficulty following certain rules or specific structures when drawing or coloring. As no one else in the family came from the creative field or loved art (including Joyce herself), the family accepted this feedback as being the truth.

However, after trying to help Janet with many other things that were safe for her, such as singing, dancing, and music, Joyce noticed that Janet's interest was still in colors. Thankfully, in 2010, Joyce finally found an art teacher who was willing to teach her. This time round, Joyce told the art teacher everything that all the previous art teachers said about Janet and told her not to repeat them as they did not interest Janet. Instead, the teacher should just see what she can do with Janet over her love for colors. Gladly, this worked. The art teacher's feedback was, "Janet has her limitations, but she has patience, and her color sense is good even though she never follows the rules!"

In 2014, under the guidance of this art teacher, Janet had her first exhibition in the United States. The Hidden Truths Project is an art exhibition where every painting was done by someone who has epilepsy. It was here that Janet's self-esteem started to grow. Her phobia that she was an epileptic left her as she saw that there were others there who had the same illness as her. She was warmly welcomed by people she didn't know, and the fact that her painting was sold even before the exhibition was opened compounded her joy.

While she produced many more beautiful paintings that were subsequently sold, Janet would continue to let her imagination and fantasy loose. In her world, a banana could be purple, and the ocean would be yellow. There were no limitations to what she could do with a paintbrush in hand. "This worried me as I always wondered why she would still do things her own way when what she learned in art class was giving her so much recognition. To me, it just tells me that something is not right. Am I going on the right path, or is she not really an artist?" These were words that kept running in Joyce's mind.

In 2017, Joyce finally found an artist who was willing to be Janet's mentor. She shared her worries with him and was assured that as an artist, he would be able to tell Joyce if Janet was a born artist once he started working with her. It was a relief when Joyce was told that Janet was a colorist. Her paintings, inspired by nature, focused on vibrant colors.

Recognition and Health Struggles

Since then, this young artist has continued to forge ahead, earning numerous accolades, including the Young Inspiring Woman Award in 2021, the NFT Superstars Award in April 2022, and the Highly Commendable Award from the International Bureau for Epilepsy (IBE) in 2023 (June).

However, fate continued to deal with her cruel blows. As Janet's star glittered brightly in art circles, both locally and internationally, her health began to deteriorate, especially after she contracted COVID-19 in December 2022. Sometime at the end of April, Janet began experiencing stomach pains, which ultimately led to her cancer diagnosis on 11 May 2023. "By the time Janet reached an unbearable state of pain and was willing to undergo a check-up, it was already at an advanced stage," Joyce recounts.

The prognosis was bleak, and Janet chose not to pursue the intensive treatment that had been recommended for her. Her concerned parents sought many second opinions from various doctors, but each one delivered the same verdict — Janet needed to undergo an invasive operation to endure punishing rounds of chemotherapy, and her health condition would make it unlikely for her to survive the aggressive treatments. Janet was 160cm height but weighed only 34kg by then. "My husband and I had to engage in yet another difficult conversation,"

Joyce says softly. "Did we want her to endure painful treatments and suffer to the end, or could we allow her to make her own choice?"

They finally agreed to let Janet decide, and she bravely chose to spend her remaining time at home. Though her body was frail, her spirit remained robust, and she wanted to live life on her own terms. In the last days before her passing, Janet was finally able to articulate her emotions. Calling out to her parents and her sister, she constantly told them the same thing: "I love you. I will always be with you. I will never leave you. We are a family."

Tears run freely down Joyce's face. "My daughter, who was never able to express her feelings, told us these words again and again."

On 7 July 2023, Janet passed away peacefully at the age of 33. We sit quietly in this space, surrounded by Janet's art.

Honoring Janet: A Tribute to Her Art and Resilience

After Janet passed on, Joyce had wanted to call it a closure after all her remaining artworks were sold. It was Janet's sister who encouraged her to carry on with the roadmap that was set up when Janet Lee Gallery opened its doors in 2020. The first of this roadmap was to offer a give-back to the society by supporting and mentoring family members of other neuro-divergent artists.

With that, the "House of Janet Lee" was launched on 7 November 2023, which coincides with Janet Lee Gallery's 3rd year anniversary.

To learn more about Janet, please visit

https://linktr.ee/artistjanetlee.

CHAPTER 3

CULTIVATING SELF-COMPASSION

Practicing Kindness and Understanding Toward Oneself, Especially in Moments of Perceived Failure

In this chapter, we delve into the essential practice of cultivating self-compassion, emphasizing the importance of showing kindness and understanding toward oneself, particularly during times of perceived failure or inadequacy.

3.1 Understanding Self-Compassion

Self-compassion is the act of treating oneself with warmth, kindness, and understanding, much like one would treat a close friend in need. It involves acknowledging one's own suffering and responding with empathy and compassion rather than self-criticism or judgment. Research has shown that cultivating self-compassion can lead to greater emotional well-being, resilience, and overall life satisfaction.

"It's okay not to be okay." This simple yet profound realization has been a guiding principle on my journey toward cultivating self-compassion. As I reflect on my experiences growing up, I recognize the moments when I felt overwhelmed by self-doubt and insecurity. I often questioned my worth and struggled to find acceptance in a world that seemed to demand perfection at every turn.

3.2 Practicing Kindness Toward Oneself

A crucial aspect of self-compassion is the practice of kindness toward oneself. This means offering oneself words of encouragement and support, especially during moments of difficulty or failure. Instead of engaging in self-criticism or negative self-talk, individuals can learn to treat themselves with gentleness and understanding, recognizing that they are worthy of compassion and care.

Practicing kindness toward oneself also involves letting go of unrealistic expectations and embracing one's imperfections as part of the human experience. By accepting oneself fully, flaws and all, individuals can cultivate a greater sense of self-acceptance and resilience.

We are human beings, and we make mistakes, fail, and learn from the lessons. This fundamental truth has been a source of comfort and empowerment as I have navigated the complexities of life. Embracing imperfection means embracing the full spectrum of human experience, including the moments of vulnerability and uncertainty that shape our growth and development.

3.3 Cultivating Understanding Toward Oneself

Another important component of self-compassion is cultivating understanding toward oneself. This involves recognizing and accepting one's thoughts, feelings, and experiences without judgment or criticism. It means acknowledging that everyone experiences moments of vulnerability and self-doubt and that these experiences are a natural part of being human.

Cultivating understanding toward oneself also means being mindful of one's own needs and desires and treating oneself with the same level of care and compassion that one would offer to others. By developing greater self-awareness and self-compassion, individuals can become more attuned to their inner experiences, leading to greater emotional resilience and well-being.

Life is never a linear curve; we have our ups and down moments, and that's what makes us a better version of ourselves, especially as women. This realization has been particularly poignant for me as I have grappled with feelings of inadequacy and self-doubt. Growing up, I often felt like I wasn't enough – not pretty enough, not smart enough, not worthy enough of love and acceptance.

As I matured and gained perspective, I have come to recognize the inherent beauty and strength in embracing life's ups and downs. Each challenge I have faced, each setback I have encountered, has been an opportunity for growth and self-discovery. Instead of viewing my imperfections as limitations, I now see them as valuable lessons that have shaped me into the person I am today.

3.4 Practicing Self-Compassion in Daily Life

Incorporating self-compassion into daily life involves making a conscious effort to prioritize self-care and self-acceptance. This may include engaging in activities that bring joy and fulfillment, such as spending time with loved ones, pursuing hobbies and interests, or practicing mindfulness and meditation.

Additionally, individuals can work on reframing negative self-talk and challenging self-critical thoughts with self-compassionate responses. Instead of berating themselves for perceived failures or shortcomings, individuals can offer themselves words of encouragement and support, recognizing their efforts and progress, no matter how small.

Seeking support from friends, family, or a therapist can also be helpful in cultivating self-compassion. By surrounding oneself with individuals who offer kindness and understanding, individuals can learn to extend the same level of compassion toward themselves, leading to greater emotional resilience and well-being.

While growing up, I always felt I was not enough; I didn't look pretty, I always got bullied, and not smart enough. These feelings of inadequacy weighed heavily on my self-esteem and confidence, leading me to question my worth and value as a person. However, through the journey of cultivating self-compassion, I've learned to challenge these negative beliefs and embrace myself with kindness and understanding.

By recognizing that it's okay not to be okay, embracing imperfection as a natural part of being human, and embracing life's ups and downs as opportunities for growth, I have found a deeper sense of self-acceptance and self-compassion. I no longer measure my worth by external standards of beauty or success but rather by the depth of my kindness, the strength of my resilience, and the authenticity of my spirit. And in doing so, I have discovered a newfound sense of empowerment and freedom to embrace myself – flaws and all – with love and compassion.

In essence, cultivating self-compassion is a journey of self-discovery and self-acceptance. By practicing kindness and understanding toward oneself, especially in moments of perceived failure or inadequacy, individuals can develop greater resilience, inner peace, and overall well-being, leading to a more fulfilling and meaningful life.

Live from
the heart
of yourself.

Seek to
be whole,
not perfect.

– Oprah

CHAPTER 4

OVERCOMING IMPOSTOR SYNDROME

Strategies for Recognizing and Combating Feelings of Inadequacy and Impostor Syndrome

In this chapter, we delve into the pervasive phenomenon known as impostor syndrome and explore practical strategies for recognizing and overcoming feelings of inadequacy and impostor syndrome. We examine how impostor syndrome manifests itself, its impact on individuals, and effective techniques for overcoming its grip.

4.1 Understanding Impostor Syndrome

Impostor syndrome, also called perceived fraudulence, involves feelings of self-doubt and personal incompetence that persist despite your education, experience, and accomplishments.

((bit.ly/3WveDOe)

Individuals experiencing impostor syndrome often attribute their achievements to luck or external factors rather than acknowledging their own abilities and efforts.

> Based on a study conducted by Psychology Today, around 25 to 30 percent of high achievers may suffer from impostor syndrome. And around 70 percent of adults may experience impostor syndrome at least once in their lifetime.
>
> **bit.ly/3Wz7LiQ**

Impostor Syndrome can manifest in various ways, including perfectionism, self-doubt, fear of failure, and a reluctance to accept praise or recognition. It can affect individuals of all backgrounds and levels of success, from students to professionals, and can have a significant impact on mental and emotional well-being.

Impostor Syndrome is a phenomenon that many individuals, including myself, may experience without even realizing it. It wasn't until I reached my 40s that I began to recognize the signs of impostor syndrome in my own life. Looking back, I can see how this insidious belief system influenced my thoughts and behaviors, often without my conscious awareness.

4.2 Recognizing the Signs of Impostor Syndrome

Recognizing the signs of impostor syndrome is the first step toward overcoming its grip. Common signs include:

1. **Persistent self-doubt:** Individuals experiencing impostor syndrome often doubt their own abilities and fear being exposed as a fraud.

2. **Perfectionism:** Individuals may set excessively high standards for themselves and feel like they must excel in every aspect of their lives.

3. **Discounting achievements:** Individuals may downplay their successes and attribute them to luck or external factors rather than acknowledging their own skills and efforts.

4. **Fear of failure:** Individuals may avoid taking risks or pursuing opportunities for fear of failure or rejection.

5. **Difficulty accepting praise:** Individuals may feel uncomfortable receiving praise or recognition for their accomplishments, believing that they do not deserve it.

In my own journey, impostor syndrome manifested in various ways. I would often find myself working on office assignments repeatedly, second-guessing my work and feeling a constant need for validation from others. I would put in countless hours on projects, striving for perfection and fearing criticism or failure. Despite my hard work and dedication, I struggled to acknowledge my own accomplishments and always felt like I didn't deserve recognition or praise.

It is important to note that by identifying these signs, individuals can start comprehending the underlying patterns of thinking and behavior that fuel impostor syndrome, allowing them to take proactive steps toward addressing them.

4.3 Combating Impostor Syndrome

Combating impostor syndrome requires a multifaceted approach that addresses both the underlying thoughts and beliefs contributing to feelings of inadequacy, as well as practical strategies for building confidence and self-assurance.

My mindset around success and worthiness was deeply influenced by impostor syndrome. I was hesitant to ask for promotions or higher pay raises, fearing that I wasn't good enough or deserving of such recognition. I harbored a belief that money was the root of all evil and that I should give more than I received, often prioritizing the needs of others over my own. This mindset kept me trapped in a cycle of self-doubt and self-sacrifice, preventing me from fully embracing my worth and potential.

Through my personal journey, I have discovered that a powerful strategy for overcoming impostor syndrome involves reframing negative self-talk and confronting self-critical thoughts with balanced and realistic perspectives. Instead of focusing on perceived failures or shortcomings, individuals can learn to recognize their strengths and accomplishments and give themselves credit where credit is due.

Additionally, setting realistic goals and expectations can help individuals break free from the cycle of perfectionism and self-doubt. By setting achievable goals and celebrating small victories along the way, individuals can build confidence and self-esteem over time.

Seeking support from friends, family, or a mentor can also be helpful in combating impostor syndrome. By sharing their experiences with trusted individuals, individuals can gain perspective and reassurance and realize that they are not alone in their struggles.

Practicing self-care and self-compassion is another important aspect of overcoming impostor syndrome. By prioritizing their own well-being and treating themselves with kindness and understanding, individuals can cultivate a greater sense of self-worth and resilience in the face of adversity.

Overcoming impostor syndrome requires a shift in mindset and a commitment to challenging negative beliefs and thought patterns. Through self-awareness and introspection, I began to recognize the ways in which impostor syndrome was holding me back and limiting my potential. I sought out support from mentors, colleagues and friends who helped me see my strengths and capabilities more clearly.

I also learned to reframe my beliefs around success and worthiness, recognizing that I am deserving of recognition and compensation for my contributions. Instead of viewing money as inherently negative, I began to see it as a tool for empowerment and impact. I embraced the idea that by valuing myself and my worth, I could make a greater difference in the world and contribute more fully to my own success and fulfillment.

In summary, overcoming impostor syndrome is a journey of self-discovery and self-acceptance. By recognizing the signs of impostor syndrome, challenging negative thought patterns, and practicing self-care and self-compassion, individuals can break free from feelings of inadequacy and impostor syndrome and realize their full potential.

"You alone are enough. You have nothing to prove to anybody."

– Maya Angelou

UNBREAKABLE SPIRIT

Suanne's Journey of Resilience, Redemption and Reborn!

Suanne Lai

I am Suanne. I'm a servant of God, a proud mom of two teenage boys, and a wife. I returned to the corporate world as a salesperson in 2023 after being a full-time homemaker for ten years and ten months.

My Childhood Journey in an Unloving Family

As a child, I was unwanted and reunited with my parents at the age of nine. While others felt parental warmth, I felt fear. Imagine being raised by grandparents and suddenly having a woman and a man claim to be your parents, and now you have to stay with them. They were strangers to me.

My first memory of my mother was her shaming me before we moved to Kedah. I had a poor classmate, Thanaletchumy, who couldn't afford color pencils. We had to color something, and I quickly finished my work and lent mine to her, telling her she could return them the next day.

I was a simple-minded child. My friend couldn't afford them and looked sad, so I loaned her my color pencils. You don't tell, I don't tell, no one knows, right?

I forgot there was a new woman in my life who called herself my mother. She appeared out of nowhere to check my school bag and found I didn't have my color pencils. She shouted, screamed, and interrogated me. I was shaking and trembling in fear. Who was she? Why was she so harsh? My grandpa never treated me this way.

"Gung Gung (Grandpa), where are you? Please take her away from me. I am scared…"

Grandpa had returned "home." He couldn't save me anymore. I spoke the truth, "I loaned it to my friend. She had no color pencils. She will return them tomorrow." My mother brought out the rotan (cane) and started to "beat" me. Not a gentle lash, but she took it all out on me. One hit… two hits… and slowly, my whole body was covered in deep cane marks.

Grandma saw it, but no one stopped her. Each hit came with a command, "Don't you dare to cry!" I was trembling in fear, in pain, but not allowed to cry. The whole family witnessed it, yet no one saved me. I stood still and let her beat me until she was satisfied over a box of STAEDTLER Luna Color Pencils (24 pieces).

I was instructed to go to my room, but no crying was allowed. Grandma suggested I skip school the next day due to the bruises on my body, but my mother insisted I had to go to school. I usually rode the school bus, but the next day, my mom arranged to send me instead.

I chose the longest dark blue pinafore, trying to cover the bruises. My mom walked me to the classroom. I was proud to finally have a "mother" and thought I could introduce her to my friends. Instead, she paraded me in front of the class, pulled up my skirt, and proudly showed my classmates my bruises. Living with my mother, I had to explain and justify all my actions. Anything that didn't please her, she punished me with the cane.

Corporate Mom: Struggles, Triumphs, and the Journey of Two Worlds

I dropped out of college because I couldn't afford the school fees. Without a degree, I had to develop a survivor's mentality to work hard and earn my place in the corporate world. I grew and earned a decent income in the company, but my life was never smooth sailing. I was often bullied, backstabbed, and taken advantage of. Those horror stories are enough to make anyone want to lash out at those ex-colleagues and bosses.

The last straw was when I had a miscarriage and fainted at home. That incident made me choose to leave the corporate world and focus on raising my two boys and taking care of my own health.

Did I leave happily? No, the truth was I didn't. On my last working day, I locked myself in the car at One World Hotel's car park and cried. I cried so much because I loved the job a lot, and yet I had to quit. It wasn't an easy decision; it's never easy to give up a good career. But I did it anyway because the workplace was toxic, and my immediate manager was toxic, too. In the car, I cried out loud, "God, forgive them, as they do not know what they were doing."

After becoming a full-time homemaker, my world gradually became smaller. While my ex-colleagues were talking about how great the world was and how exciting the multi-million deals were, my topics revolved around groceries and kids. Slowly, I withdrew from everyone, and eventually, I fell into depression.

Depression...

Depression seems to be an illusion, a fabricated mental state. Suanne cried for help, but no one took her seriously. Suicidal thoughts loomed daily, and she battled with them every single day for many years. Her salvation was her two children; they kept her alive and loved her deeply.

Whenever the pain became unbearable, suicidal thoughts would haunt me. I thanked God for having my two sons beside me, who hugged and kissed me whenever I was down and in a state of depression. The battle had been ongoing for a couple of years. I would lock myself in the room, asking God, "Why me? What have I done wrong, God? What have I done to anger You so badly?"

My perspective changed over the years, and I started to be thankful and grateful. I changed my conversation with God to, "God, I thank you for the depression. I may not understand why, but if I can praise You during my good days, I will also praise You during my bad days. May I know what lesson You want me to learn?" Slowly and gradually, as I drew closer to God and thanked Him on a daily basis, practicing gratitude instead of complaining, I grew happier and healed from my depression.

Second Act: Rediscovering Purpose After a Career Pause

After ten years and ten months, due to the rising cost of living, I had no choice but to return to the workforce. My goal is simple: to do whatever it takes to pay the bills and my kids' school fees. It wasn't an easy journey; ten years and ten months was not a small gap. Throughout those years, I tried to re-enter the corporate world. Each rejection made my world feel smaller and smaller, to the point where I thought it was impossible to even take up a backend administrative role.

Being a woman isn't easy, and being a working mom in the corporate world is even harder. I've had my fair share of unpleasant experiences as a young mother. I've faced discrimination, and due to my long career break, I was seen as "unhireable" in the eyes of hiring managers. I felt small and believed there was no way for me to return to the corporate world. I thought I was destined to spend my life as a housewife, doing daily chores and taking care of my kids.

With God's grace, here I am, back to where I used to be, standing strong again, finding my way to start building my foundation in the corporate world. Even though I am earning 50% less than what I used to in my previous employment, I need to earn my right to rise in the corporate world to regain my credibility, both professionally and financially.

Where is my Next Path?

I am in a stage of confusion in my life, trying to figure out a lot of things. There are days when I smile and laugh, and there are days when I am sad and crying. This is my genuine human side.

While I am still finding myself and working hard to stay relevant in the current world, I am finding the strength to take up leadership roles and serve. At my current job, I am a first-time manager and wanted to bring out the best in my assistant, helping her find her path and supporting her throughout her professional journey.

Outside of work, I have started volunteering on community projects related to women's empowerment. I have been selected as a member of the ISC2 Malaysia Chapter Sub Committee of Women Empowerment. My plan is to build my strength to gather my people and rise together. This is how I want to serve the community.

My message for women: "Hello, you are not alone. There are many of us who face similar challenges like you. Let us journey together. Let us rise together! Life is short. Let us make it a worthwhile journey."

CHAPTER 5

SETTING BOUNDARIES AND ASSERTING YOURSELF

Assertiveness Training and Boundary-Setting Techniques to Foster Self-Respect and Confidence

In this chapter, we explore the critical importance of setting boundaries and asserting oneself in fostering self-respect and confidence. We delve into the principles of assertiveness training and provide practical techniques for establishing and maintaining healthy boundaries in various aspects of life.

5.1 Understanding Boundaries

Setting boundaries is crucial for maintaining healthy relationships and preserving our well-being. However, like many others, I have struggled with setting boundaries myself. For years, I found myself saying yes to every request or favor without considering the impact on my own mental and physical health. This pattern of people-pleasing took a toll on me, particularly during the Covid-19 pandemic when the demands on my time and energy seemed endless.

The consequences of overextending myself became clear when I experienced burnout and exhaustion. I realized that by constantly saying yes to others, I was neglecting my own needs and neglecting to acknowledge my own emotions. It was a wake-up call that prompted me to take a step back and reevaluate my approach to setting boundaries.

Boundaries are the physical, emotional, and psychological limits that define the parameters of acceptable behavior in relationships and interactions. Healthy boundaries are essential for maintaining self-respect and preserving one's well-being. They enable individuals to communicate their needs and preferences effectively, while also respecting the needs and boundaries of others.

Setting boundaries involves clearly communicating one's limits and expectations to others and taking action to enforce those boundaries when necessary. This can involve saying "no" to requests or demands that are unreasonable or infringe upon one's autonomy, as well as advocating for one's needs and preferences in a respectful and assertive manner.

I made a conscious decision to prioritize self-care and assertiveness in my interactions with others. Instead of automatically saying yes to every request, I began to pause and consider whether it aligned with my own values and priorities. I reminded myself that I didn't have to please everyone and that it was okay to prioritize my own well-being.

5.2 Assertiveness Training

Assertiveness training is a form of communication skills training that focuses on teaching individuals how to express their thoughts, feelings and needs assertively while also respecting the rights and boundaries of others. Assertive communication involves expressing oneself clearly, confidently, and respectfully without resorting to aggression or passivity.

Key principles of assertiveness training include:

1. **Self-awareness**: Understanding one's own needs, feelings, and boundaries is essential for effective assertive communication. By developing greater self-awareness, individuals can identify their priorities and preferences and communicate them assertively to others.

2. **Active listening**: Listening actively and empathetically to the perspectives of others is an important aspect of assertive

communication. By demonstrating genuine interest and understanding, individuals can build rapport and mutual respect in their interactions.

3. **"I" statements**: Using "I" statements to express thoughts, feelings, and needs can help individuals communicate assertively without blaming or accusing others. By taking ownership of their own experiences, individuals can convey their message more effectively and avoid defensiveness or conflict.

4. **Assertive body language:** Nonverbal cues such as eye contact, posture, and facial expressions play a crucial role in assertive communication. Assertive body language conveys confidence, openness, and respect, helping individuals establish credibility and authority in their interactions.

5.3 Boundary-Setting Techniques

Effective boundary-setting involves a combination of assertive communication skills and self-awareness. Some practical techniques for setting and maintaining boundaries include:

1. **Identifying personal values and priorities:** Clarifying one's values and priorities can help individuals determine which boundaries are most important to

them and guide their decision-making in setting and enforcing boundaries.

2. **Communicating clearly and directly**: Clearly expressing one's boundaries and expectations to others is essential for effective boundary-setting. Using assertive communication techniques, such as "I" statements and active listening, can help individuals communicate their needs and preferences in a respectful and confident manner.

3. **Saying "no" when necessary**: Learning to say "no" to requests or demands that are unreasonable or do not align with one's values is an important aspect of boundary-setting. Confidently asserting one's right to decline offers or invitations can help individuals protect their time, energy, and resources.

4. **Setting consequences for boundary violations**: Establishing consequences for boundary violations can help individuals enforce their boundaries and deter others from engaging in disrespectful or inappropriate behavior. Consequences should be clear, consistent, and proportionate to the violation and communicated assertively to the other party.

5. **Seeking support when needed:** Seeking support from trusted friends, family members, or professionals can provide validation, encouragement, and guidance in setting and maintaining boundaries. By surrounding themselves with a supportive network, individuals can gain confidence and strength in asserting themselves and protecting their well-being.

Embracing assertiveness involves learning to communicate my needs and boundaries clearly and respectfully. I started to practice assertive communication techniques, such as using "I" statements and expressing myself assertively but empathetically. I also learned to say no without guilt or apology, knowing that my self-respect and well-being were worth prioritizing.

Navigating responses to boundaries can be challenging, especially when others react negatively to our assertiveness. However, I've come to realize that true friends will respect and support our boundaries, even if they don't always agree. I've learned to prioritize relationships that are built on mutual respect and understanding rather than on people-pleasing or codependency.

As such, setting boundaries and asserting oneself is essential for fostering self-respect, confidence, and healthy relationships. By learning assertiveness training techniques and boundary-setting strategies, individuals can communicate their needs and preferences effectively while also respecting the rights and boundaries of others.

By prioritizing self-care, practicing assertiveness, and prioritizing relationships that honor our boundaries, we can cultivate self-respect, confidence, and resilience in our interactions with others. And in doing so, we create space for authentic connections and meaningful relationships that nourish and support us on our journey.

"I don't need anyone's permission to feel glorious."

DEVELOPGOODHABITS.COM

CHAPTER 6

NAVIGATING LIFE TRANSITIONS WITH CONFIDENCE

Strategies for Maintaining Confidence During Significant Life Changes

In this chapter, we explore the challenges of navigating life transitions and provide strategies for maintaining confidence during periods of change, such as career shifts, relationship changes, or parenthood. We delve into the psychological and emotional aspects of transitions and offer practical techniques for building resilience and self-assurance.

6.1 Understanding Life Transitions

Life transitions are inevitable parts of the human experience, marked by significant changes in one's circumstances, roles, or identities. Whether it's starting a new job, starting or ending a relationship, or becoming a parent, transitions can evoke a range of emotions, including excitement, anxiety, and uncertainty.

Transitions can challenge our sense of identity and purpose, forcing us to adapt to new roles and responsibilities. They can also disrupt our routines and habits, leading to feelings of instability and insecurity. However, transitions also present opportunities for growth and self-discovery, allowing us to redefine ourselves and pursue new goals and aspirations.

Growing up in a large family with limited resources, I learned the value of resilience and resourcefulness from an early age. With seven siblings and a few luxury items, our childhood was marked by simplicity and creativity. Instead of toys, we found joy in simple pleasures like playing by the river, climbing trees, and engaging in outdoor activities. Despite our modest circumstances, I cherished the bonds formed with my siblings and the sense of connection we shared.

My quiet nature and preference for solitude followed me into my school years, where I gravitated toward a few close friends rather than large crowds. While I struggled to navigate social situations, I found solace and joy in the company of my trusted companions. With them, I could chat and laugh freely, allowing my true self to shine without reservation.

6.2 Maintaining Confidence During Transitions

Maintaining confidence during transitions requires a combination of self-awareness, adaptability, and resilience. Some strategies for building confidence during periods of change include:

1. **Embracing uncertainty:** Recognizing that change is a natural part of life can help individuals approach transitions with greater resilience and openness. Embracing uncertainty and viewing transitions as opportunities for growth and learning can help individuals navigate change with confidence and optimism.

2. **Setting realistic expectations**: Setting realistic expectations for oneself during transitions can help alleviate pressure and reduce feelings of anxiety or self-doubt. Recognizing that it's okay to make mistakes and that progress may be gradual can foster a sense of self-compassion and acceptance during times of change.

3. **Seeking support:** Seeking support from friends, family members, or professionals can provide validation, encouragement, and guidance during transitions. By surrounding oneself with a supportive network, individuals can gain perspective

and reassurance and realize that they are not alone in their struggles.

4. **Practicing self-care:** Practicing self-care and self-compassion is essential for maintaining confidence and well-being during transitions. Engaging in activities that nourish and replenish oneself, such as exercise, meditation, or spending time in nature, can help individuals manage stress and maintain a positive outlook during times of change.

5. **Focusing on strengths:** Focusing on one's strengths and past successes can help individuals build confidence and resilience during transitions. By reflecting on past accomplishments and recognizing one's abilities and talents, individuals can approach new challenges with greater self-assurance and determination.

6.3 Strategies for Specific Life Transitions

Different life transitions may present unique challenges and opportunities for growth. Some strategies for navigating specific transitions with confidence include:

a. **Career shifts:** When navigating career shifts, it's important to clarify one's values, interests, and goals and seek opportunities that align with these priorities. Building a strong support network, seeking mentorship, and continuing to invest in one's professional development can also help individuals navigate career transitions with confidence.

As I entered my twenties and ventured into the world of work, I faced new challenges and responsibilities. With a desire to support my family and secure a better future, I took on a side hustle to increase my income. Despite the demanding workload, I remained steadfast in my commitment to providing for my younger brother's education and striving for a better life for myself.

b. **Relationship changes:** Relationship changes, such as breakups or divorces, can be emotionally challenging and may impact one's sense of self-worth and confidence. It's important to prioritize self-care and seek support from friends, family, or a therapist during these transitions. Practicing self-compassion, setting boundaries, and focusing on personal growth can also help individuals navigate relationship changes with confidence and resilience.

In my thirties, societal expectations weighed heavily on me as I navigated the complexities of romantic relationships. Despite two failed relationships, I refused to let disappointment define me. Instead, I found solace and purpose in my role as an aunt, cherishing the precious moments spent with my nieces and nephews. Their laughter and innocence brought light to my life, reminding me of the joy that exists beyond romantic endeavors.

c. **Parenthood:** Parenthood brings significant changes in roles, responsibilities, and priorities, which can be both rewarding and challenging. It's important for new parents to prioritize self-care, seek support from their partner, friends, or family members, and communicate openly about their needs and concerns. Setting realistic expectations, practicing patience, and embracing the joys of parenthood can help individuals navigate this transition with confidence and grace.

Parenthood, while not a personal experience for me, has been a significant aspect of my life through my relationships with my nieces and nephews. Despite not having children of my own, I have had the privilege of watching my friends embark on the journey of parenthood. As their children transition from childhood to adulthood, I've witnessed both the challenges and joys that come with raising a family.

I've learned valuable lessons from observing the experiences of others. I've learned the importance of patience, resilience, and unconditional love in navigating life's transitions. Whether as a parent, aunt, or friend, embracing life's journey with confidence and grace means embracing the joys and challenges that come with each new chapter, knowing that every experience is an opportunity for growth and connection.

Life is full of twists and turns, and navigating its transitions requires resilience, adaptability, and self-compassion. Despite the challenges I have faced, I have emerged stronger and more resilient, armed with the knowledge that true happiness comes from within. By embracing life's ups and downs with confidence and grace, I continue to forge my path with courage and determination, knowing that every experience, whether joyful or painful, contributes to my growth and resilience as a woman.

Navigating life transitions with confidence requires self-awareness, adaptability, and resilience. By embracing uncertainty, setting realistic expectations, seeking support, practicing self-care, and focusing on strengths, individuals can navigate transitions with confidence and resilience and emerge stronger and more resilient on the other side.

this version of me
wasn't built
overnight

this is experience
and pain

this is insecurities
and abuse

this is depression
and a climb out of
rock bottom

i had to go through
a lot of shit to get to
where i am now

amazingmemovement.com

FROM STRUGGLE TO STRENGTH

A Journey to Holistic Health and Happiness

Chen Wai Ling

A Daughter's Journey

In a busy city where life never slows down, my days are full of hustle and bustle. But during all the chaos, there's one person who shapes every part of who I am: My Mom.

She's more than just a parent to me; she's my mentor, my best friend, and my rock. I've always been amazed by how she handles her job in the corporate world. She is always busy, but she never lets it get in the way of taking care of our family. No matter how tough things get, she always puts us first.

Her days are filled with meetings, deadlines, and lots of responsibilities, but she faces it all with strength and a smile. She's like a superhero to me, never backing down from any challenge.

Following her example, I found my own path in the corporate world. Heading the Human Resources and Procurement department, assisting and working closely with my mom in the plastic packaging manufacturing industry, and on the surface, everything seems great. But deep down, I feel like something's missing.

Even though I have a good job and financially stable, there's this emptiness inside me that I can't shake. I have everything I thought I wanted, but it's like there's a puzzle piece missing from my life.

A Heartbreaking Loss

In the midst of her busy life, my mom never slowed down. She was always rushing from work to home, taking care of everyone without ever complaining. But in all the hustle and bustle, she forgot to take care of herself. She hardly ever took time off for herself, maybe just a week-long holiday once a year if we were lucky.

Then, everything changed in 2013 when she was diagnosed with advanced stage Breast Cancer. It felt like the ground was ripped out from under us. Suddenly, my mom's world was filled with doctor's appointments, chemo treatments, and endless hospital visits. And amidst it all, I became her main caregiver, trying to balance my job with taking care of her.

Watching her battle with cancer was heart-wrenching. Despite her strength and resilience, I could see her health deteriorating day by day. The medical bills piled up, but no amount of money could bring back her health. It was a helpless feeling seeing my superhero mom struggling with something she couldn't control.

Then, in 2017, I still remember vividly during Mother's Day, she passed away peacefully. The loss was devastating, leaving a hole in my heart that I thought would never heal. It was a harsh reminder of just how precious life is and how quickly everything can change.

Finding Strength in Pain

Following in my mother's footsteps, I dove headfirst into the corporate world, eager to prove myself and make her proud. I worked long hours, often skipping meals to meet deadlines and ensure everything ran smoothly. But amidst the chaos, I made sure to carve out time for myself, hitting the gym to destress and unwind.

However, life had other plans for me. During my mother's cancer diagnosis, I experienced severe spine degeneration at the C6 and C7 levels. Suddenly, without any prior symptoms, I found myself unable to move from the neck down several times. I genuinely thought I was paralyzed. The pain was unbearable, and I found myself wearing a cervical collar just to get through the day. The doctors recommended surgery, but I was determined to avoid it at all costs. Instead, I turned to alternative treatments like physiotherapy, acupuncture and rehabilitation, desperate for relief so I could take care of my mom without worrying her more.

Despite all my efforts, the pain persisted, and I had to depend on painkillers to get me through the day. And when my mother passed away, it felt like the universe was testing me in ways I never thought possible. Amid my grief, I realized that I needed to prioritize my own health and well-being. I couldn't continue to ignore the signs my body was giving me.

Embracing Self-Care

Desperate to find relief from the relentless pain of my spine injury, I embarked on a journey to reclaim my health and vitality. I scoured the internet for solutions, attended countless seminars and tried various therapies, hoping to find something that would ease my suffering.

In my quest for healing, I stumbled upon the world of fitness and nutrition. Determined to take control of my health, I enrolled in courses to become a certified personal trainer. I embraced a new way of eating, making sure to nourish my body with wholesome foods and never skipping meals again. I have successfully lost 5kg, 7.8% body fat and increased my muscle mass with improved energy and strength.

I also dove headfirst into strength training, pushing myself to new limits and challenging my body to become stronger. Slowly but surely, I noticed a difference. The pain that had once consumed me began to diminish, replaced by a newfound sense of strength and resilience.

My breakthrough was nothing short of miraculous, and even my doctor was amazed by my progress. They encouraged me to continue doing what I was doing, and I took their advice to heart. I made my health a top priority, making sure to fuel my body with nutritious food and feed my soul with activities that brought me joy.

As a single person, I knew that I had to take good care of myself. I vowed to pursue happiness with the same fervor that I pursued my health, embracing every opportunity for adventure and exploration. I developed a love for travel and enjoyed jetting off to destinations around the world, soaking in new experiences and creating memories that would last a lifetime.

Sharing My Journey

Regaining my health has been nothing short of life changing. It's given me a newfound sense of purpose and a burning desire to help others on their own journey to wellness. So, I made the decision to become a wellness and fitness coach.

But this new path wasn't without its challenges. My family couldn't understand why I would want to pursue a career in health and fitness coaching when I was already financially stable. They questioned why I would want to sacrifice my free time to help others reclaim their health. Their doubts weighed heavily on me, but deep down, I knew that this was where my heart truly belonged.

Transitioning from holding a senior position in corporate, where I was accustomed to giving orders to subordinates, to becoming a wellness and fitness coach has been a profound shift. In my previous role, leadership often meant directing others and making decisions from a position of authority.

However, as a wellness and fitness coach, my approach has had to evolve significantly. I've had to learn humility, embrace a role where serving others, and listen attentively to clients' pain points, which are paramount. Each prospect brings unique challenges and goals, requiring personalized solutions rather than one-size-fits-all directives. This transition has been humbling yet incredibly rewarding, reshaping my perspective on leadership and service in profound ways.

I'm always upgrading myself through workshops and seminars to learn more and gain experience. I put in late hours every day to make the most of my time and give my best. It's not always easy, but I keep pushing myself out of my comfort zone to grow and get better at what I do.

This journey has taken me from being a learner to becoming a fitness host and speaker, where I share life insights and run coaching programs that cater to different needs. I help people achieve their health goals like losing weight sustainably and gaining healthy muscle. I've even had the opportunity to collaborate with other fitness brands, which allows me to reach and empower more people.

Ultimately, my goal is to offer a holistic transformation, focusing on both physical fitness and mental well-being. Through this journey, I find immense satisfaction in witnessing my clients, especially women who play many roles, discover new hope, confidence, and joy as they evolve into their best selves.

Setting Goals and Making a Difference

In 2022, I co-founded the Impact Zone Fitclub with four other coaches to spread wellness and fitness. Having already transformed over 100 lives across Malaysia, Macau, the UK, Australia, and Thailand in the past six years, I aimed to impact 50 more lives, especially women aged 40 and above, by my 50th birthday in 2024.

But that wasn't enough for me. I wanted Impact Zone Fitclub to make an even bigger difference. So, we set our sights on changing the lives of 1000 people through our community. It was a daunting challenge, but my determination was unwavering. I believed in the power of transformation and knew that with hard work and dedication, we could achieve anything.

Through my journey, I've learned that true beauty radiates from within. It's not just about appearance but how you feel inside. I wanted to spread this message far and wide. With courage and resolve, I embraced the belief that anything is possible.

A Message of Hope

My journey has taught me a vital lesson: Health is Wealth. Without good health, money loses its meaning. This truth hit home with my late mom, whose hard-earned income was swallowed by medical bills. I urge you, the reader, to take action now. Don't wait for the perfect moment—start taking care of yourself today. Poor health casts a shadow not only on your life but also on your loved ones, emotionally and financially.

Make self-care your priority. Believe in yourself, and don't let anyone undermine your worth. You are capable of incredible things, and you deserve to feel confident and happy because you are worth it.

Remember, there's no such thing as an ugly person. We all have our own unique beauty, and it's up to us to embrace it. Be fearless and go after your dreams. Make it your life-long mission to take care of your health so you can enjoy your best life with your family and loved ones.

As for me, I have big plans. I want to expand my business and community beyond Malaysia so that I can help even more people transform their lives. Because I truly believe that everyone deserves to live their best life, full of health, happiness, and fulfillment.

So, to anyone reading this, know that even in your darkest moments, there is always hope. By prioritizing self-care and believing in yourself, you can overcome any obstacle and live life to the fullest. I'm cheering for you, and I know that you have the strength and radiance within you to achieve anything you set your mind to.

Dedication

To my beloved mom, who remains a guiding light in my life even though you are no longer with us, this story is a tribute to our cherished memories and the profound impact you had on me. Your love, wisdom, and strength continue to inspire me every day.

To my dad, whose unwavering support and love have been my foundation.

To my brother, for always being by my side through thick and thin.

To my sister-in-law, for her kindness and for being a wonderful addition to our family.

And to my nephews, whose laughter and joy bring light into our lives.

With all my love and gratitude, Wai Ling

To follow Wai Ling's journey, please visit:

bit.ly/3Yve6ON

CHAPTER 7

BODY POSITIVITY AND SELF-IMAGE

Techniques for Developing a Healthy Relationship with One's Body and Reframing Societal Beauty Standards

In this chapter, we explore the concept of body positivity and self-image, focusing on techniques for developing a healthy relationship with one's body and challenging societal beauty standards. We delve into the impact of media and cultural influences on body image and offer practical strategies for cultivating self-love and acceptance.

7.1 Understanding Body Positivity

Body positivity is a movement that promotes acceptance and appreciation of all body types, regardless of shape, size, or appearance. It challenges societal norms and beauty standards that perpetuate unrealistic ideals of beauty and encourages individuals to embrace their bodies as they are.

Body positivity is about cultivating self-love and acceptance and recognizing that worth and value are not determined by physical appearance. It involves shifting the focus from external appearance to internal qualities and strengths and celebrating the diversity and uniqueness of the human body.

7.2 Challenging Societal Beauty Standards

Societal beauty standards, perpetuated by media, advertising, and popular culture, often promote narrow and unattainable ideals of beauty. These standards can have damaging effects on individuals' self-esteem and body image, leading to feelings of inadequacy, shame, and self-doubt.

Challenging societal beauty standards involves recognizing the harmful impact of these standards on individuals' mental and emotional well-being and actively working to counteract them. This may involve questioning unrealistic beauty ideals, advocating for greater diversity and representation in media and advertising, and promoting self-acceptance and self-love.

7.3 Techniques for Developing a Healthy Relationship with One's Body

Developing a healthy relationship with one's body requires self-awareness, self-compassion, and a willingness to challenge negative thought patterns and beliefs. Some techniques for cultivating body positivity and self-love include:

1. **Practicing self-care**: Engaging in activities that nourish and replenish the body, mind, and spirit can help individuals develop a greater sense of self-worth and appreciation for their bodies. This may include activities such as exercise, meditation, spending time in nature, or engaging in creative pursuits.

2. **Cultivating gratitude:** Practicing gratitude for one's body and its abilities can help individuals develop a greater appreciation for their physical selves. Focusing on what the body can do, rather than how it looks, can shift the focus from appearance to functionality and foster a sense of gratitude and acceptance.

3. **Surrounding oneself with positive influences:** Surrounding oneself with positive influences, such as supportive friends, family members, and role models, can help reinforce a positive body image and self-image. Seeking out communities and spaces that celebrate diversity and promote body positivity can also be empowering and affirming.

4. **Challenging negative self-talk:** Challenging negative self-talk and replacing

it with more positive and affirming messages can help individuals build self-confidence and self-esteem. This may involve reframing negative beliefs about one's body and appearance and focusing on internal qualities and strengths.

7.4 Embracing Self-Love and Acceptance

I delve into my personal journey of grappling with body image, which has been multifaceted and challenging. During my teenage years, my face was full of pimples, adding another layer of self-consciousness and insecurity. The presence of acne caused me to retreat further into myself, often hiding away at home to avoid scrutiny and judgment over my appearance.

This experience compounded with my already present feelings of being "skinny, tall, and ugly," creating a deep-seated sense of inadequacy and self-doubt. The societal pressure to adhere to narrow beauty standards only exacerbated these feelings, making it difficult to feel confident and comfortable in my own skin.

Throughout university, the struggle continued, with roommates exemplifying the pervasive obsession with weight and appearance. Witnessing their fixation on daily weigh-ins served as a stark reminder of the constant scrutiny women face regarding their bodies.

However, amidst these challenges, I began to realize the importance of self-acceptance and self-compassion. I recognized that true beauty transcends external appearance and lies in embracing one's unique qualities and strengths. Through self-reflection and inner work, I started to cultivate a more positive relationship with my body, learning to appreciate and love myself for who I am, pimples and all.

It took me many years of intentional work in progress to shift my mindset and accept myself. This journey toward body positivity and self-acceptance has been transformative, empowering me to embrace my uniqueness and live authentically, free from the constraints of societal beauty standards.

Body positivity entails embracing self-love and acceptance, acknowledging that all bodies deserve love and respect. By challenging societal beauty norms, prioritizing self-care, fostering gratitude, surrounding oneself with positive influences, and combating negative self-talk, individuals can nurture a healthier connection with their bodies and foster deeper self-love and acceptance.

In summary, body positivity is a voyage of self-discovery and self-acceptance. By embracing diversity, defying societal beauty ideals, and embracing self-love and acceptance, individuals can forge a healthier bond with their bodies, fostering heightened self-confidence and self-worth.

30-Second Confidence Boost

* Stand up straight

* Smile

* Make eye contact

* Speak clearly and directly

* Don't worry about what other people think

* Repeat any time your confidence lags

CalmHealthySext.com

CHAPTER 8

FINDING YOUR VOICE

Building Assertiveness and Effective Communication Skills to Express Oneself Authentically

In this chapter, we explore the journey of finding your voice, focusing on developing assertiveness and effective communication skills to express yourself authentically. We delve into the importance of speaking your truth and offer practical strategies for building confidence and assertiveness in communication.

8.1 The Journey of Finding Your Voice

Finding your voice is a deeply personal journey of self-discovery and self-expression. It involves uncovering your values, beliefs, and passions and learning to communicate them confidently and authentically. Finding your voice empowers you to assert your needs, boundaries, and aspirations and advocate for yourself and others.

However, this journey can be challenging, particularly in environments where conformity and compliance are valued over individuality and authenticity. It requires self-awareness, courage, and a willingness to embrace vulnerability and uncertainty.

8.2 Building Assertiveness and Effective Communication Skills

Building assertiveness and effective communication skills is essential for finding your voice and expressing yourself authentically. Assertiveness involves expressing your thoughts, feelings and needs confidently and respectfully while also respecting the rights and boundaries of others. Effective communication involves listening actively, expressing yourself clearly, and fostering understanding and connection in your interactions.

Some strategies for building assertiveness and effective communication skills include:

1. **Practicing self-awareness:** Developing self-awareness is key to assertiveness and effective communication. Take time to reflect on your values, beliefs, and emotions, and consider how they influence your thoughts, behaviors, and interactions with others.

2. **Setting boundaries:** Setting boundaries is essential for assertiveness and self-care.

Clearly communicate your boundaries to others and assertively enforce them when necessary. Remember that it's okay to say no to requests or demands that do not align with your values or priorities.

3. **Using assertive language:** Use assertive language to express yourself confidently and respectfully. Use "I" statements to communicate your thoughts, feelings, and needs, and avoid apologizing or minimizing your opinions or preferences.

4. **Active listening:** Actively listen to others' perspectives and experiences and respond empathetically and non-judgmentally. Show genuine interest and curiosity in what others have to say and seek to understand their viewpoints before expressing your own.

5. **Seeking feedback:** Seek feedback from trusted friends, family members, or mentors on your communication style and assertiveness. Be open to constructive criticism and use it as an opportunity for growth and learning.

6. **Practicing assertiveness in everyday situations:** Practice assertiveness in everyday situations, such as asking for what you need, expressing your opinions and preferences, and asserting your boundaries.

Start with small, low-stakes interactions and gradually build your confidence and assertiveness over time.

By building assertiveness and effective communication skills, you can find your voice and express yourself authentically in all areas of your life. Whether it's asserting your needs and boundaries, advocating for yourself and others, or expressing your passions and beliefs, developing these skills empowers you to live authentically and make a positive impact in the world.

I explore my journey of finding my voice amidst the challenges of being introverted and soft-spoken. Throughout my career, I often found my voice ignored or overlooked, leading to feelings of frustration and invisibility. However, as I rose up the ranks and assumed managerial positions, I learned the importance of assertiveness and effective communication in gaining recognition and influence.

Despite being naturally introverted, I realized that speaking up didn't necessarily mean raising my voice or being aggressive. Instead, it involved cultivating assertiveness and firmness in expressing my thoughts and opinions. By mastering the art of assertive communication, I found my voice heard and respected in professional settings, empowering me to advocate for myself and others with confidence and conviction.

Through practice and perseverance, I honed my assertiveness skills, learning to assert my boundaries, communicate my ideas effectively, and navigate challenging conversations with poise and clarity. This transformation not only bolstered my confidence and self-esteem but also enhanced my leadership abilities, enabling me to inspire and empower others to find their own voices in the workplace.

As such, finding my voice was a journey of self-discovery and empowerment, requiring courage, resilience, and a commitment to personal growth. By embracing assertiveness and effective communication, I transcended the limitations of introversion and soft-spokenness, reclaiming my power and influence in the professional arena.

"One of the criticisms I've faced over the years is that I'm not aggressive enough or assertive enough, or maybe somehow, because I'm empathetic, I'm weak. I totally rebel against that. I refuse to believe that you cannot be both compassionate and strong."

JACINDA ARDERN

BRAVING THE JOURNEY

A Daughter's Quest for Love, Purpose, and Empowerment

Lolitta Suffian

I was from a family of four: my father, mother, younger brother, and myself, the eldest. Dad worked as a chemical engineer in an oil and gas company, spending two weeks offshore and two weeks at home. Our family was like many traditional Asian families, where sons were cherished more than daughters. When I was born, my mother felt disappointment; she showered all her love on my younger brother, believing boys deserved more attention.

From a young age, I was taught that my role as a girl was to manage the household, cook well, find a good husband, and settle down as a dutiful wife. My education wasn't a priority for my mother, who never acknowledged my achievements even though I was doing well in my studies. Despite this, I found solace and support from my father, who always stood by my decisions.

In the Asian community context, these gender roles were deeply ingrained. Boys were groomed to be the main breadwinners, while girls were groomed to be homemakers and caretakers. The expectations for girls like me were clear: excel in domestic skills, be submissive to a future husband, and prioritize family over personal aspirations. Education and career were often seen as secondary options, a mere stepping stones to securing a suitable marriage rather than avenues for personal fulfillment.

These societal norms shaped not only my family dynamics but also my early ambitions. While I excelled academically, my achievements were often overshadowed by my brother's successes, reinforcing the belief that his future was more important. Despite my love for art and dreams of higher education, I faced constant discouragement from my mother, who saw little value in pursuits outside traditional gender roles.

However, amidst these challenges, my father's unwavering belief in my potential became my beacon of hope. He encouraged me to pursue my passions and supported my decision to study for a Diploma in Fine Art and Graphic Design. His belief in equality and opportunity, despite societal pressures, instilled in me the courage to challenge norms and carve out a path that honored both tradition and personal ambition.

A Journey of Passion: Embracing Art and Self-Discovery

I find immense joy in studying at an Arts College in Ipoh, where I can truly explore and expand my artistic talents while embracing my individuality. Thereafter, I eagerly pursued further education in the USA to broaden my horizons. Yet, my dreams were cut short due to overwhelming financial constraints, forcing me to make the heartbreaking decision to return to Malaysia. Upon returning, I relocated to Kuala Lumpur in search of job opportunities.

In Kuala Lumpur, I embarked on my first career in the hotel industry. It was an exhilarating time, stepping into the world of hospitality, where each day presented new challenges and chances for personal growth. Securing my first job was more than just about earning a pay cheque; it signified newfound independence and the liberty to chart my own course in life.

I vividly remember the sense of accomplishment and excitement that came with receiving my first salary. It was a validation of years of hard work and dedication to my studies and personal development. For the first-time, I had the financial means to support myself and make decisions based on my own aspirations and goals.

Amidst this newfound independence, I unexpectedly met someone who would change my life. Within just three months of courtship, I made the impulsive decision to marry him. My father, the pillar of wisdom and support, questioned if this was truly what I wanted. The sweet memories of the early days of our courtship, despite not really knowing him well, lured me into believing I could escape my past and forge my own path. With my parent's blessings, I embarked on starting my own family.

Struggles and Sacrifices: Balancing Passion with Motherhood

Marriage brought new challenges and responsibilities. My job in the hotel industry demanded considerable time, often keeping me at work late evenings and weekends. On the other hand, I have to keep up with house chores and attend to my husband's needs.

Over time, my then-husband requested that I transition to a more conventional job. Subsequently, I found a new role as an Art Facilitator at Wings of Creativity, a subsidiary of Lim Kok Wing University. Teaching art became my passion, as creativity and all things art-related truly resonated with me. However, the position required weekend work, which strained our relationship. Accustomed to a more traditional lifestyle, my husband felt embarrassed when I couldn't always be present, especially during gatherings with friends and family over the weekend.

He never showed interest or cared to understand the challenges I faced, whether at work or at home. As the head of the household, he expected me to be a submissive wife, prioritizing house chores and his needs above all else.

Despite our differences, I was determined to make the marriage work. When I became pregnant, my husband insisted that I quit my job to focus on our growing family. Shortly after, he lost his job, plunging us into a financial crisis. We depleted our savings and turned to his mother for help, but her limited resources as a single parent offered little relief.

In desperation, jobless and struggling, I had to swallow my pride and seek assistance from my father. It was humbling to admit our predicament, knowing my father had his own responsibilities to manage. With his unwavering support, we navigated through the immediate financial turmoil, yet tensions within our family continued to escalate.

Months passed with no job prospects for my husband, intensifying the strain at home. His frustration often erupted into anger directed at me. Despite being pregnant, I summoned the courage to seek employment to support my family financially. I found solace working at a kindergarten franchise, where I could channel my energy into nurturing young minds and creating educational illustrations. Designing colorful visuals and writing workbooks for children became a source of joy and purpose amidst the turmoil. On top of that, I was blessed with the kindness of my Canadian boss and his wife. Their understanding and encouragement bolstered me during this challenging time.

Despite my efforts to maintain peace, the atmosphere at home grew increasingly volatile. My husband's wounded pride from our financial dependence on me and my commitment to my career fueled his resentment. His mother, a staunch traditionalist, exacerbated tensions with relentless criticism of my homemaking skills and perceived failures as a wife.

Breaking Point: Escaping Darkness for Motherhood's Sake

During a big fight at my mother-in-law's place, things got really bad. My husband, overwhelmed by his own anger and insecurities, threatened to throw my son, Adam, off the balcony unless I bowed down and apologized to him and his mother. In that terrifying moment, all I could think about was keeping my son safe.

With a heavy heart and shaky hands, I knew I had to leave. Adam was just eight months old, nestled tightly in my arms as I quietly packed our essentials while my husband slept. Fear and uncertainty filled my mind, but my determination to give my son a stable, safe home gave me strength. Early in the morning, tears streaming down my face, I called my dad, pouring out my heart and asking for his help once again.

Without hesitation, my dad came to rescue us. His calm and unwavering support was a ray of hope in the midst of chaos. With his guidance, I started rebuilding my life as a single mom. We moved away from the troubles of my failed marriage but stayed connected to my dad, who was always there for me.

Rebuilding Amidst Adversity

The road ahead was daunting, filled with legal battles and emotional turmoil as we navigate the complexities of divorce under Shariah Law. Despite the challenges, every step forward was a testament to my resilience and determination to create a better future for Adam and myself.

After my decision to seek a divorce, I faced the first hurdle at the police station. My plea for a police report detailing my husband's abuse was met with dismissal by a male officer who deemed it a private family matter. Deflated but not defeated, I turned to my father for guidance. His unwavering support and encouragement propelled me to try again. This time, fate intervened in the form of a compassionate female officer who listened attentively to my ordeal and ensured the report was filed.

With the police report in hand, I proceeded to the Shariah Court to initiate the divorce proceedings. The bureaucratic process was rigorous, beginning with mandatory counseling sessions aimed at reconciling marital disputes. However, my husband refused to acknowledge the irreconcilable differences, adamantly opposing the divorce. His mother, a staunch advocate of traditional values, added to the turmoil with hurtful accusations and disparaging remarks.

For two arduous years, I persevered through hearings, negotiations, and emotional confrontations. Finally, the divorce was granted. It was a bittersweet victory, marking the end of a painful chapter but also the beginning of a new journey toward healing and renewal. With my father's unwavering support and Adam's innocent smile as my driving force, I embraced the future with cautious optimism.

A New Beginning: Embracing Love and Renewal

Along the journey, my determination never faltered. I held a steady job as a customer service officer at a contact center in Kuala Lumpur, where each day brought new challenges and a sense of purpose. Meanwhile, Adam stayed in Ipoh under my father's loving care, and every weekend, I traveled from Kuala Lumpur to Ipoh to cherish the precious moments with my son.

Amid echoes of past struggles, a new chapter began with my current husband. We were married after two years of courtship. His arrival marked a turning point—a beacon of hope after the darkness of my failed marriage.

We met unexpectedly in the hustle of Kuala Lumpur. He was from Singapore, his warmth and kindness drawing me in effortlessly. Our initial talks were filled with shared interests and mutual respect, laying the foundation for a deepening bond.

Unlike my rushed past, our relationship grew slowly, built on understanding and genuine companionship. He listened to my journey, respecting its complexities while encouraging me to envision a brighter future. His patience and unwavering support were a stark contrast to my previous tumultuous experiences.

We navigated cultural differences and personal histories with open hearts, determined to create a nurturing environment for our blended family. His acceptance of Adam as his own son and dedication to fostering a loving relationship filled me with gratitude and renewed hope.

Our marriage became a testament to love's healing power and the human spirit's resilience. While we've had our fair share of arguments, we've always made a point to communicate and reconcile. Each day, we grew individually and as a family, cherishing lessons from our journeys. Our home became a sanctuary—a place where laughter, understanding, and unconditional love flourished, transcending past shadows.

Through it all, my husband became not just my partner but also my confidant and ally. I was blessed with the 19th year of marriage with him in 2024. His belief in my strength fueled my aspirations, empowering me to make a positive impact in my community. Together, we embraced the joys and challenges of parenthood, nurturing Adam and our children with love and guidance.

Rising Strong: From Survival to Leadership and Legacy

Today, we've built a family together, and I've found fulfillment in mentoring young women through various projects in Malaysia. Volunteering as a mentor for "Project Girls 4 Girls Malaysia" has been particularly rewarding. This Harvard-born nonprofit organization empowers young women with courage, vision, and skills to take on public leadership roles.

Through this initiative, I strive to instill in them the same resilience and determination that guided me through my own challenges. By sharing my story and experiences, I hope to inspire them to break free from societal constraints and pursue their dreams with confidence.

Additionally, I am honored to mentor under "Aspire," a program by Telekom Malaysia aimed at developing future leaders within the company. This role allows me to contribute shaping the next generation of managers and executives, fostering an environment where talent is recognized and nurtured.

Legacy of Love: Honoring My Father's Guidance and Leadership

Reflecting on my journey, I credit my late father for the guiding light through my darkest times and inspiring me to empower others. My father was more than just a parent—he was my rock, my mentor, and my biggest supporter. His support remains my foundation, reminding me always to be brave in facing life's challenges and nurturing future leaders. His belief in my potential continues to resonate in my work as I strive to create opportunities for the young generation to thrive and excel in their chosen fields.

My mission goes beyond professional success; it's about creating a legacy of empowerment and leadership. Through mentorship and advocacy, I aim to break down barriers and promote gender equality in leadership roles. Each interaction with a mentee reaffirms my commitment to fostering a supportive and inclusive community where women can flourish and make meaningful contributions to society.

CHAPTER 9

BUILDING A
SUPPORTIVE NETWORK

The Importance of Surrounding Oneself with Positive Influences and Cultivating Supportive Relationships

In this chapter, we explore the significance of building a supportive network and the vital role it plays in personal and professional growth. We delve into the impact of surrounding oneself with uplifting individuals and nurturing connections and provide practical strategies for cultivating a supportive network.

9.1 Understanding the Power of Supportive Networks

A supportive network consists of individuals who uplift, encourage, and inspire us to be our best selves. These individuals may include friends, family members, mentors, colleagues, and community members who provide emotional support, guidance, and encouragement. A supportive network serves as a source of strength and resilience during challenging times and a catalyst for personal and professional growth.

9.2 The Importance of Positive Influences

Positive influences play a crucial role in shaping our beliefs, attitudes, and behaviors. Surrounding oneself with positive influences can boost self-esteem, foster optimism, and promote a sense of belonging and connection. Positive influences provide validation, encouragement, and constructive feedback, helping us develop confidence and resilience in pursuing our goals and aspirations.

9.3 Cultivating Supportive Relationships

Cultivating supportive relationships involves intentional effort and investment in nurturing connections with others. This may include:

1. **Building trust and mutual respect:** Trust and respect are the foundation of any supportive relationship. Building trust involves being reliable, honest, and transparent in your interactions, while respect involves honoring each other's boundaries, perspectives, and autonomy.

2. **Communicating openly and honestly:** Open and honest communication

is essential for fostering understanding and connection in relationships. This involves expressing oneself authentically and listening actively and empathetic to others' perspectives and experiences.

3. **Offering and seeking support:** Supportive relationships involve reciprocity, with both parties offering and receiving support as needed. This may involve providing emotional support, practical assistance, or simply being present and available when needed.

4. **Celebrating successes and milestones:** Celebrating successes and milestones, both big and small, is an important aspect of cultivating supportive relationships. This involves acknowledging and celebrating each other's achievements and milestones and offering encouragement and validation along the way.

9.4 Strategies for Building a Supportive Network

Some strategies for building a supportive network include:

1. **Identifying positive influences:** Take stock of the individuals in your life and identify those who uplift, encourage, and inspire you. Cultivate relationships with these individuals and prioritize spending time with them.

2. **Seeking out supportive communities:** Join groups, clubs, or organizations that align with your interests and values and provide opportunities for connection and support. These communities can serve as a source of camaraderie, inspiration, and encouragement.

3. **Being proactive in nurturing connections:** Take initiative in reaching out to others and building meaningful connections. Whether it's through social gatherings, networking events, or one-on-one conversations, foster relationships with individuals who share your goals and aspirations.

4. **Being a supportive presence:** Be a supportive presence in the lives of others by offering encouragement, validation, and assistance when needed. Show up for others in times of need and celebrate their successes and milestones with genuine enthusiasm and joy.

In summary, building a supportive network is essential for personal and professional growth, resilience, and well-being. By surrounding themselves with positive influences and cultivating supportive relationships, individuals can find strength, encouragement, and inspiration to navigate life's challenges and pursue their dreams and aspirations with confidence and resilience.

I delve into the significance of building a supportive network and finding my tribe amidst life's challenges and triumphs. Throughout my journey, I have discovered the invaluable role that various support groups play in nurturing my growth and well-being.

One of the pillars of my support network is my church community, where I find solace, guidance, and spiritual nourishment. Here, I am embraced by a community of like-minded individuals who share my values and provide unwavering support through life's ups and downs.

Another crucial pillar of my support system includes my close friends from various stages of life—school, university, and the workplace. These trusted companions provide empathy, understanding, and a shoulder to lean on in times of need. My family plays another integral role in supporting me through life's challenges. Their unwavering presence serves as a constant reminder that I am never alone in my journey.

Additionally, I have found a sense of belonging and empowerment within a non-governmental organization (NGO) dedicated to women's empowerment. Here, I am surrounded by passionate individuals committed to uplifting and advocating for women's rights and equality. Through this community, I draw inspiration, strength, and solidarity as I navigate the challenges of womanhood and strive to make a positive impact in the world.

By cultivating relationships within these diverse support groups, I've created rich connections that uplift and empower me to be the best version of myself. These relationships serve as a source of encouragement, validation, and motivation, reminding me of my inherent worth and potential. In embracing my tribe, I've discovered the power of community in shaping my journey and fostering resilience, growth, and fulfillment.

CHAPTER 10

SUSTAINING CONFIDENCE FOR A LIFETIME

Tips and Practices for Maintaining and Strengthening Confidence as Women Navigate Different Stages of Life

In this chapter, we explore the importance of sustaining confidence throughout a lifetime, particularly for women, as they navigate various stages of life. We provide practical tips and practices for maintaining and strengthening confidence, empowering women to face life's challenges with resilience and self-assurance.

10.1 Understanding the Importance of Confidence

Confidence is a crucial asset that empowers women to pursue their goals, overcome obstacles, and fulfill their potential. It provides a foundation of self-assurance and resilience, enabling women to navigate life's ups and downs with grace and determination. Sustaining confidence throughout a lifetime is essential for fostering personal and professional growth, maintaining well-being, and achieving fulfillment and success.

10.2 Tips for Maintaining Confidence

Some tips for maintaining confidence as women navigate different stages of life include:

1. **Cultivating self-awareness:** Develop a deep understanding of yourself, including your strengths, values, and aspirations. Self-awareness enables you to make informed decisions, set realistic goals, and navigate challenges with confidence and clarity.

2. **Embracing resilience:** Embrace challenges as opportunities for growth and learning. Cultivate resilience by reframing setbacks as temporary obstacles rather than insurmountable barriers. Learn from failures and setbacks and use them as stepping stones toward greater success and fulfillment.

3. **Prioritizing self-care:** Make self-care a priority in your daily routine. Take time to nurture your physical, emotional, and mental well-being through activities such as exercise, meditation, and relaxation. Practice self-compassion and self-kindness and treat

yourself with the same level of care and respect that you would offer to others.

4. **Seeking support:** Surround yourself with supportive friends, family members, mentors, and colleagues who uplift, encourage, and inspire you. Lean on your support network during challenging times and celebrate your successes and milestones with those who share in your joy and accomplishments.

5. **Continuing to learn and grow:** Embrace a growth mindset and commit to life-long learning and personal development. Stay curious and open-minded and seek out opportunities for growth and exploration. Invest in your education, skills, and passions, and pursue opportunities that challenge and inspire you to reach your full potential.

10.3 Practices for Strengthening Confidence

Some practices for strengthening confidence include:

1. **Positive self-talk:** Cultivate a positive internal dialogue and challenge self-limiting beliefs and negative thought patterns. Replace self-doubt with affirmations and encouragement, and remind yourself of your strengths, accomplishments, and potential.

2. **Visualization:** Use visualization techniques to imagine yourself succeeding in various aspects of your life. Visualize yourself overcoming challenges, achieving your goals, and living a fulfilling and meaningful life. Visualization can help build confidence and motivation and pave the way for success in your endeavors.

3. **Goal setting:** Set clear, achievable goals that align with your values and aspirations. Break down large goals into smaller, manageable steps, and celebrate your progress along the way. Goal setting provides focus and direction and empowers you to take action toward creating the life you desire.

4. **Stepping outside your comfort zone:** Challenge yourself to step outside your comfort zone and embrace new opportunities for growth and exploration. Pushing past your fears and limitations builds resilience and confidence and expands your horizons in ways you never thought possible.

5. **Practicing gratitude:** Cultivate an attitude of gratitude and appreciation for the blessings and opportunities in your life. Take time each day to reflect on the things you are grateful for and express gratitude to yourself and others. Gratitude fosters a sense

of abundance and fulfillment and enhances overall well-being and confidence.

In essence, sustaining confidence for a lifetime requires self-awareness, resilience, self-care, support, and a commitment to growth and development. By implementing practical tips and practices for maintaining and strengthening confidence, women can navigate life's challenges with grace, resilience, and self-assurance and embrace the journey of personal and professional fulfillment with confidence and courage.

I've embraced sustaining and strengthening my confidence throughout my journey. Recognizing the importance of continuous self-development, I enrolled myself in self-development programs and immersed myself in books focused on confidence and positivity. Through intentional efforts, I sought out positive-minded communities and support groups that fostered a culture of encouragement and empowerment.

One pivotal step in my confidence-building journey was distancing myself from negative influences. I recognized the draining effect of negativity on my energy and well-being, prompting me to consciously limit my exposure to negative people and environments. By surrounding myself with positivity and uplifting influences, I created a conducive environment for growth and self-improvement.

Moreover, I embraced a proactive approach to nurturing my confidence, incorporating daily practices and gratitude that bolstered my self-esteem and resilience. From affirmations and visualization exercises to setting and achieving personal goals, I committed myself to cultivating a mindset of empowerment and self-belief.

Through these concerted efforts, I've not only sustained my confidence but also experienced transformative growth and fulfillment. As I continue to navigate the various stages of life, I draw strength from the practices and communities that support my journey of self-discovery and empowerment. By prioritizing my well-being and investing in my personal growth, I've cultivated a deep sense of confidence that serves as a guiding light, empowering me to thrive and flourish in every aspect of my life.

A Confident Woman

I am Strong

I've been through a lot in my life and I'm still standing.

I have Self-Worth

It took a lot of soul searching to finally see for myself.

I am not Perfect

I don't need anyone to tell me, I already know my glow.

I am Beautiful

Nobody's perfect, but I've seen my good and bad sides.

I am just Myself

I will never be alone, I will always be there for me!

a place for mom

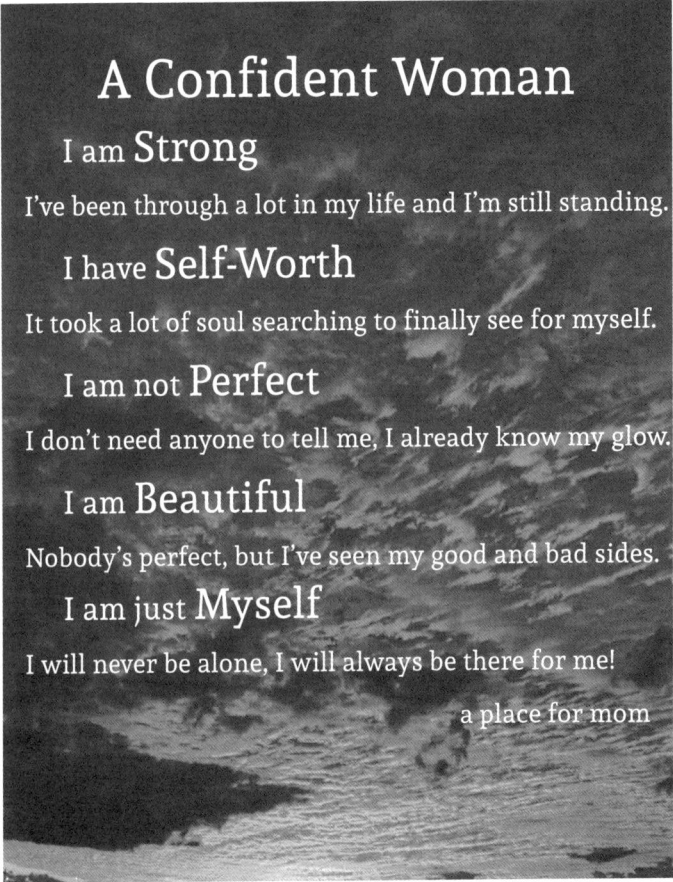

ABOUT THE AUTHOR

L ian Wai Bee is a seasoned marketer whose journey into writing has been shaped by a diverse career spanning over 30 years in marketing management. Her transition from corporate leadership to passionate social advocacy underscores her dedication to driving positive change and cultivating a more equitable world for women everywhere.

The onset of the COVID-19 pandemic served as a catalyst for Wai Bee's pivot towards making a meaningful social impact. Motivated by a desire to contribute and learn deeply, she found herself drawn to "Project Girls 4 Girls," a Harvard-born NGO dedicated to empowering young women with the vision, courage, and skills essential for leadership roles.

Mentoring within "Project Girls 4 Girls" ignited a profound purpose within Wai Bee. Guiding and supporting young women nurtured their potential and fostered their leadership capabilities, prompting her to delve deeper into human psychology to forge meaningful connections with those around her.

Inspired by these transformative experiences, Wai Bee embarked on a compelling journey to write a book amplifying women's voices and shedding light on the challenges they courageously navigate. Her book aims to showcase the resilience and fortitude of women, fostering unity and empowerment in overcoming barriers with unwavering strength.

In her exploration, Wai Bee encountered the silent struggles of women career returnees who often felt unworthy and penalized for their hiatus. Many faced significant obstacles, including being offered salaries nearly 50% lower than their previous earnings, despite their skills and experience. This disparity fuelled her determination to advocate for fair treatment and support for women re-entering the workforce.

Through her writing and continued mentorship, Wai Bee exemplifies her belief in the power of community and collective action. Her commitment to mentoring girls into courageous leaders and advocating for the rights of women career returnees reflects her vision of a more inclusive and supportive world.

PRAISE FOR LIAN WAI BEE'S

Embracing Imperfections, Women's Stories of Triumph

"Embracing Imperfections: Women's Stories of Triumph not only comes with stories of triumph, it also includes invaluable anecdotes about discovering and achieving that triumph. It's definitely a Highly Recommended guide for women looking for answers to navigate the challenges in their lives."

– Jennifer Fernandez, Assistant VP ELMU Group and Published Author

"Embracing Imperfections: Women's Stories of Triumph is a book to inspire all women out there to stay confident in sailing through life trajectory. The four touching real-life stories that resonate with the readers are very impactful in offering strength and hope. As a research enthusiast in women's studies, I highly recommend this book for all women to read"

– Daphne Lim, Assistant Professor, Edinburgh Business School, Heriot-Watt University Malaysia

"*Embracing Imperfections: Women's Stories of Triumph,* the book's personal stories are beautifully written, taking me on an emotional roller coaster. I caught myself smiling, tearing up, and feeling deeply INSPIRED. One of the key take away for me, each person is on their own journey, both the good and bad experiences that shape who we become"

– Aida Azman, Chapter Section Lead, Delivery Management, Roche

"*Embracing Imperfections: Women's Stories of Triumph.* What makes this book truly stand out for me are the four real-life stories of Malaysian women, from different ages and backgrounds. These women's voices bring the book to life, showing us what resilience really looks like. Their experiences show us that we can overcome anything with determination and grit".

– Chuah Ai Jou – Writer & Editor, Marketing Communications

"*Embracing Imperfections: Women's Stories of Triumph.* Sometimes life's challenges are hard. I understand and feel for everyone with their stories shared in the book. The women I am today is purely because of all life's challenges that were thrown to me without being prepared. Love this"…accepting the imperfections gives you freedom". The book is not meant for everyone but it is meant for women who are ready to embrace it all."

- Anonymous